RAND

A Description of U.S. Enlisted Personnel Promotion Systems

Stephanie Williamson

Prepared for the
Office of the Secretary of Defense

National Defense Research Institute

Preface

This report describes the enlisted personnel promotion systems used by the Army, Navy, Marine Corps, and Air Force during the early to mid-1990s. The report should be of interest to anyone seeking a brief overview of the services' promotion criteria in the 1990s.

Although the report is descriptive and not meant to assess or analyze the services' promotion systems, the report also serves as an important reference for recent RAND research on the quality of enlisted personnel. In that research, a new measure of personnel quality is being developed. The new measure, based on an application and extension of earlier work done at RAND (Ward and Tan, 1985), develops a quality index that depends on entry characteristics as well as an unobserved quality factor. Empirical estimation of the new quality measure requires information about a service member's first-term promotion outcomes, and, to ensure confidence that differences in promotion outcomes correspond to meaningful differences in personnel quality, a description of the services' promotion systems becomes essential. The material presented in this report supports the notion that the services' promotion criteria are related to key aspects of personnel quality, including duty performance, leadership potential, experience, knowledge, and skills and therefore that promotion outcomes do correspond to substantive differences in personnel quality. Finally, the reader should recognize that the services occasionally revise their promotion systems, and therefore, information on the very latest promotion rules and regulations should be obtained directly from the services.

The related reports on quality are:

> Hosek, James R., and Michael G. Mattock, *Measuring the Quality of Enlisted Personnel in the U.S. Armed Forces*, Santa Monica, Calif.: RAND, forthcoming.

> Asch, Beth J., John T. Warner, James R. Hosek, Michael G. Mattock, *Recruiting, Retaining, and Promoting High Quality Personnel: Towards Understanding the Adequacy of the Military's Compensation and Promotion Systems*, Santa Monica, Calif.: RAND, forthcoming.

This research was conducted for Personnel and Readiness within the Forces and Resources Policy Center of RAND's National Defense Research Institute, a federally funded research and development center sponsored by the Office of the

Secretary of Defense, the Joint Staff, the unified commands, and the defense agencies.

Contents

Appendix

Figures

Tables

Summary

This document summarizes the requirements for promotion of enlisted personnel within each of the services of the U.S. military. This document is not a historical review and does not assess or evaluate the promotion systems. Furthermore, this document does not address the enlisted promotion systems used for the reserves.

There is marked variety in the specific requirements for promotion across services. However, there is similarity in the tiered structure of the services' promotion systems. For example, each service developed a tiered enlisted promotion system (Figure S.1). Basically, the first level of the promotion systems controls the promotion of enlisted personnel up to paygrades E-3/E-4. At this level, advancement is noncompetitive and requirements are minimal; generally enlisted personnel need only meet time-in-service (TIS) and time-in-grade (TIG) requirements for advancement. The middle tier covers a wider range of enlisted personnel between paygrades E-4 and E-5/E-7 with competitive advancement based primarily on point systems. The advancement requirements in the top level vary across services. However, at this level, promotion decisions are made primarily by board reviews.

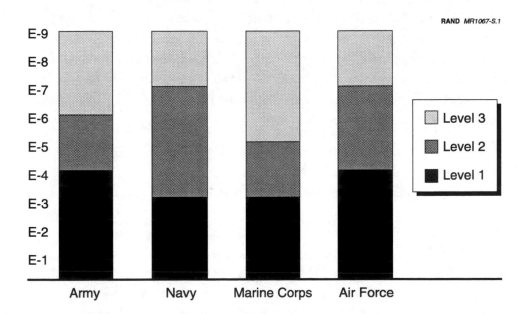

RAND *MR1067-S.1*

Figure S.1—Promotion System Structure Levels

The first level of the enlisted promotion system within the active-duty Army is a decentralized system that promotes soldiers to grades through specialist (E-4) based on unit commanders' authorization and TIS and TIG requirements. The second level, the semicentralized system based primarily on a point system, promotes to the grades of sergeant and staff sergeant (E-5 and E-6). The third level, centralized promotions, promotes enlisted personnel to sergeant first class through sergeant major (E-7 to E-9) by board review action.

The Navy enlisted promotion system is based primarily on a point system; however, advancement to general apprenticeship, apprentice (E-2), and general apprenticeship (E-3) necessitates meeting TIG and TIS requirements. In addition to TIG and TIS requirements, advancement to E-3 requires passing an apprentice and naval standards examination. Advancement to petty officer, third class (E-4), through chief petty officer (E-7) is dependent on obtaining requisite promotion points. Promotions to senior chief petty officer (E-8) and master chief petty officer (E-9) do not require examinations. However, commanding officer's recommendation is required as well as selection board action.

Like the Navy, the Marine Corps has no point requirements for promotion up to the grade of E-3. Promotions to corporal (E-4) and sergeant (E-5) are authorized on the basis of vacancies existing throughout the Marine Corps and are effected by authorized commanders. Promotions are based on automatic composite scores (CS), which are computed quarterly for each eligible lance corporal (E-3). The CS is based on a variety of performance factors: rifle marksmanship, physical fitness, duty performance, conduct, and education. Advancement to staff sergeant through master gunnery sergeant and sergeant major (E-6 to E-9) requires recommendation from the selection boards, which convene annually. Achievement, leadership, professional and technical knowledge, military proficiency, and physical fitness are just a few items considered by the selection board when making promotion decisions.

The Air Force enlisted promotion system is based primarily on skill levels and a point system. In addition to the TIG requirement, promotions to airman (E-2) and airman first class (E-3) are normally noncompetitive and require recommendation from commanders. In addition to TIG and TIS requirements, airmen first class (E-3) must be recommended by their unit commander and must have a 3-skill level to be eligible for promotion to senior airman (E-4). (See Section 5 for a discussion of skill levels.) Promotions to the grades of staff sergeant through master sergeant (E-5 through E-7) occur under one of two programs: the Weighted Airman Promotion System (WAPS) or Stripes for Exceptional Performers (STEP). WAPS is an objective promotion system based on points received in six weighted categories, and STEP is a promotion system that allows for the advancement of airmen with exceptional potential. Finally, consideration for promotion to senior master sergeant (E-8) and chief master sergeant (E-9) is a two-phase process consisting of WAPS factors and a central evaluation board at Headquarters, Air Force Military Personnel Center (HQAFMPC), using the whole-person concept.

The services' promotion systems are discussed separately in detail in the main sections of this document.

TIS and TIG requirements are the basic requirements for promotion. The minimum TIS requirement, established by the Department of Defense (DoD), is usually achieved automatically when the TIG requirement is met. Tables S.1 and S.2 compare the TIS and TIG requirements across the services. Additionally, Table S.1 compares the DoD guidelines for the desired and minimum TIS requirements for promotion eligibility against the TIS criteria set by the services. The Navy is the only service to adhere to the DoD-desired TIS requirement for promotion to all grades.

Table S.1

Minimum Time-in-Service Requirements

Promotion to	DoD-Desired	DoD Minimum	Army[a]	Navy	Marine Corps	Air Force
E-2	6 months	Active-Duty Entry	6 months	6 months	6 months	NA
E-3	12 months	Active-Duty Entry	12 months	12 months	9 months	NA
E-4	2 years	6 months	26 months	2 years	12 months	36 months
E-5	3 years	18 months	3 years	3 years	24 months	3 years
E-6	7 years	4 years	7 years	7 years	4 years	5 years
E-7	11 years	6 years	6 years	11 years	6 years	8 years
E-8	16 years	8 years	8 years	16 years	8 years	11 years
E-9	19 years	10 years	10 years	19 years	10 years	14 years

[a]With maximum waiver for E-2 through E-4 and secondary zone for E-5 and E-6.
SOURCES: Army Regulation 600-8-19, 1 November 1991 with Interim Change I01, 8 April 1994. BUPERSINST 1430.16D, 1991. MCO P1400.32.B, 1996. Air Force Pamphlet 36-2241, Volume 1, 1 July 1995. DoD Directive 1304.20, 1984.

Table S.2

Minimum Time-in-Grade Requirements

Promo- tion to	Army	Navy	Marine Corps	Air Force
E-2	6 months	9 months	6 months	6 months
E-3	4 months	9 months	8 months	10 months
E-4	6 months	6 months	8 months	20 months or 28 months
E-5	8 months	12 months	12 months	6 months
E-6	10 months	36 months	27 months	23 months
E-7		3 years	3 years	24 months
E-8		3 years	4 years	20 months
E-9		3 years	3 years	21 months

SOURCES: Army Regulation 600-8-19, 1 November 1991 with Interim Change I01, 8 April 1994. BUPERSINST 1430.16D, 1991. MCO P1400.32.B, 1996. Air Force Pamphlet 36-2241, Volume 1, 1 July 1995.

Acknowledgments

I thank James Hosek for his perceptive guidance and constructive reviews, Harry Thie for his insightful review and useful suggestions for improving the report, and Beth Asch for her helpful comments and suggestions on earlier versions of this report. Any errors included in this report are solely my responsibility.

Abbreviations

AFS	Air Force Specialty
AFSC	Air Force Specialty Code
ANCOC	Advanced Noncommissioned Officers' Course
APR	Airman Performance Report
BNCOC	Basic Noncommissioned Officers' Course
BUPERS	Bureau of Personnel (Navy)
BUPERSINST	BUPERS Instruction
CEM	Chief Enlisted Manager
CMF	Career Management Field
CNO	Chief of Naval Operations
CPMOS	Career progression military occupational specialty
CS	Composite score
DOR	Date of rate
EDAS	Enlisted Distribution and Assignment System
EMF	Enlisted master file
EPR	Enlisted Performance Report
ESR	Enlisted Summary Record
FMS	Final multiple score
GMP	General Military Proficiency
HQDA	Headquarters, Department of the Army
HYT	High Year Tenure
IEMF	Inactive enlisted master file
MCI	Marine Corps Instruction
MCTFS	Marine Corps Total Force System
MOS	Military occupational specialty
NAVSTD	Naval Standards
NEAS	Navy Enlisted Advancement System
OccFld	Occupational Field
OCCSTD	Occupational Standards

ODCSPER	Office of the Deputy Chief of Staff for Personnel
OJT	On-the-job training
PAFSC	Primary Air Force Specialty Code
PARs	Personnel advancement requirements
PECD	Promotion eligibility cutoff date
PERSCOM	U.S. Total Army Personnel Command
PFE	Promotion Fitness Examination
PFT	Physical fitness test
PLDC	Primary Leadership Development Course
PMA	Performance Mark Average
PMOS	Primary military occupational specialty
PNA	Passed but not advanced
RI	Reporting Identifier
SDI	Special Duty Identifiers
STEP	Stripes for Exceptional Performers
TAFMS	Total Active Federal Military Service
TIG	Time-in-Grade
TIR	Time-in-Rate
TIS	Time-in-Service
TOPCAP	Total Objective Plan for Career Airmen Personnel
WAPS	Weighted Airman Promotion System

1. Introduction

This document describes the enlisted personnel promotion system used by each of the four services of the U.S. military. This document is not a historical review and does not assess or evaluate the promotion systems. Similarities exist between the services' promotion system structures. However, there is variety in the procedures and requirements for advancement across services.

Section 2 through Section 5 of this document describe the enlisted personnel promotion systems used by the Army, Navy, Marine Corps, and Air Force, respectively.

2. Army Enlisted Promotion

The Army's enlisted promotion system "provides for career progression and rank that is in line with potential, recognizing the best qualified soldier that will attract and retain the highest caliber soldier for a career in the Army." (AR 600-8-19, 1991.)

Each month the Department of the Army establishes the total number of soldiers to be promoted based on budgetary and strength constraints. The number of promotions is allocated by primary military occupational specialty (PMOS).

The Army enlisted promotion system is divided into three sections: decentralized, semicentralized, and centralized.

Decentralized Promotions

Decentralized promotions through specialist (E-4) are managed by unit commanders using the Enlisted Distribution and Assignment System (EDAS). Commanders are authorized to advance soldiers to the grade of specialist (E-4) and below. Furthermore, soldiers are only advanced in their PMOS or career progression military occupational specialty (CPMOS).

Advancement to Private E-2 (E-2)

Advancement to private E-2 requires the commander's authorization and six months TIS and TIG (Table 2.1). The TIS requirement can be waived up to four months.

Advancement to Private First Class (E-3) and Specialist (E-4)

Advancement to private first class requires the commander's authorization, 12 months TIS, and four months TIG (Table 2.1). Up to six months TIS and two months TIG may be waived.

For advancement to specialist, there is a 26-month TIS and a six-month TIG requirement with up to 12 months TIS and three months TIG that can be waived. Soldiers holding PMOS in Career Management Field (CMF) 18 (Special Forces)

Table 2.1

Minimum TIG and TIS Requirements for Promotion Within the Army

Promotion to		TIG	TIG Waiverable Months	TIS	TIS Waiverable Months
Private	E-2	6 months		6 months	4 months
Private First Class	E-3	4 months	2 months	12 months	6 months
Specialist	E-4	6 months	3 months	26 months	12 months
Sergeant	E-5	8 months	4 months	3 years	18 months
Staff Sergeant	E-6	10 months	5 months	7 years	36 months
Sergeant First Class	E-7			6 years	
Master Sergeant	E-8			8 years	
Sergeant Major	E-9			10 years	

SOURCE: Army Regulation 600-8-19, 1 November 1991 with Interim Change I01, 8 April 1994.

with 18 months TIS and recommended by a promotion board, or Ranger School graduates with at least 12 months TIS, may be advanced to specialist without regard to TIG.

Semicentralized Promotions

Promotions to sergeant (E-5) and staff sergeant (E-6) are managed in a semicentralized procedure. Field operations (board appearances, promotion point calculation, promotion list maintenance, and execution of the promotion) are decentralized, and Headquarters, Department of the Army (HQDA), operations are centralized. Monthly, HQDA determines and announces promotion point cutoff scores by grade for each military occupational specialty (MOS) on the basis of the scores reported by the field and the needs of the Army. In October 1995, the U.S. Total Army Personnel Command (PERSCOM) implemented a new system, the EDAS, for management of semicentralized enlisted promotions. EDAS provides a real-time update of points and grades at HQDA and allows for instant error feedback notification.

Soldiers compete for promotion against all other eligible soldiers in their primary MOS and zone. There are two promotion zones for enlisted personnel: primary and secondary. The primary zone consists of soldiers of a specified grade whose date of rate (DOR) falls within the announced zone of consideration and who meet promotion requirements.[1] The secondary zone provides outstanding soldiers with later DOR whose accomplishments, demonstrated capability for

---

[1] Approximately four months prior to the convening date of each selection board, HQDA establishes and announces the zones of consideration for each selection board. The zones define the DOR requirements for consideration by the selection board in either the primary zone or the secondary zone.

leadership, and marked potential an opportunity to compete for advancement ahead of their peers. With waivers, TIS and TIG requirements in the secondary zone are considerably less than those in the primary zone. For example, for a sergeant (E-5) competing for promotion to staff sergeant (E-6) the TIS and TIG requirements for advancement in the primary zone are 84 months and 10 months, respectively, and in the secondary zone with the maximum waivers are 48 months and five months, respectively (Table 2.2).

In December 1995, a procedural change was implemented to simplify the way points are added and changed and how grade changes are processed. Annual submission of the promotion point worksheet is no longer mandatory for soldiers; however, soldiers are required to validate their promotion eligibility list standing within a 24-month period from their last recomputation, reevaluation, or initial board appearances. Furthermore, a minimum of 20 points is required for an administrative reevaluation (McHugh, 1996; Milper Message 96-213).

The promotion point worksheet is used to recommend a soldier for promotion or reevaluation, or to request that the information be used in the next recomputation of promotion points. The commander completes section A (Recommendation) of the promotion point worksheet and sends the form to the promotion authority. TIS and TIG criteria for promotion can be waived. The soldier's most recent assigned weapon qualification (expert, sharpshooter, marksman) and the most recent physical fitness test scores (situps, pushups, two-mile run) are recorded in section A. (A copy of the promotion point worksheet is in Appendix C.)

Semicentralized advancement to sergeant (E-5) and staff sergeant (E-6) is based on the total of administrative points and board points. Table 2.3 summarizes the areas and maximum points per category. Administrative points are based on duty performance,[2] awards and decorations (Appendix B, Table B.1), military and civilian education, and military training. The military education requirements direct that soldiers competing for promotion to E-5 must be graduates of the Primary Leadership Development Course (PLDC) prior to being promoted,[3] and soldiers competing for promotion to E-6 must be graduates of the PLDC prior to being recommended for promotion and must be graduates of the Basic Noncommissioned Officers' Course (BNCOC) to be promoted. The civilian educational criterion requires a high school diploma, general education development (GED) equivalent, or higher degree. Military training points are based on marksmanship and physical fitness.

---

[2]Duty performance points (a maximum of 200 points) are awarded by the soldier's commander.
[3]Soldiers can compete for promotion to E-5 without completion of the PLDC.

Table 2.2

Army Primary and Secondary Zone TIG and TIS Requirements for Promotion

Promotion to		TIG		TIS	
		Primary Zone	Secondary Zone[a]	Primary Zone	Secondary Zone[a]
Sergeant	E-5	8 months	4 months	36 months	18 months
Staff Sergeant	E-6	10 months	5 months	84 months	48 months

[a]With maximum waiver.
SOURCE: Army Regulation 600-8-19, 1 November 1991 with Interim Change I01, 8 April 1994.

Board points are based on the promotion selection board's evaluation of the soldier. Promotion boards, consisting of at least three voting and one nonvoting members, are conducted on the fifteenth of each month. In a question-and-answer format, the board evaluates the soldier in the following areas: personal appearance, bearing, and self-confidence; oral expression and conversational skill; knowledge of world affairs; awareness of military programs; knowledge of basic soldiering; and soldier's attitude, which includes leadership and potential for advancement and trends in performance. The promotion selection board scores the soldier in each area listed above in one of four categories: average, above average, excellent, or outstanding. The points awarded for each category vary. For example, the maximum score for an outstanding rating range from 25 to 45 points. The maximum total awarded by the board is 200 points. Soldiers must be recommended by a promotion selection board for advancement.

Advancement to Sergeant (E-5)

Recommendation by the soldier's unit commander begins the promotion process for semicentralized promotions. The TIS requirement for attaining eligibility for promotion to sergeant is 36 months Active Federal Service for the primary zone and 18 months for the secondary zone. The TIG requirement for attaining eligibility for promotion to sergeant in either primary or secondary zone is eight months as a corporal or specialist. Waivers up to four months are permissible for TIG. Soldiers in the secondary zone may be boarded with 15 months TIS. As of October 1989, soldiers competing for promotion to sergeant (E-5) must be graduates of the PLDC prior to being promoted.

In addition to TIS, TIG, and education requirements, the minimum promotion point score for attaining recommended list status for promotion to sergeant is 450 points.

Table 2.3

**Total Promotion Points for Promotion to Sergeant
and Staff Sergeant (E-5 and E-6)**

Item	Maximum Points	
	Sergeant	Staff Sergeant
Duty Performance	200	200
Skill Qualification Test	*	*
Awards and Decorations	50	50
Military Education	150	150
Civilian Education	100	100
Military Training	100	100
Total Administrative Points	600	600
Total Board Points	200	200
Total Promotion Points	800	800

SOURCE: Army Regulation 600-8-19, 1 November 1991 with Interim Change I01, 8 April 1994.

Advancement to Staff Sergeant (E-6)

The TIS requirement for attaining eligibility for promotion to staff sergeant is 84 months Active Federal Service for the primary zone and 48 months for the secondary zone. The TIG requirement for attaining eligibility for promotion to staff sergeant is 10 months as a sergeant. Waivers of five months are permissible for TIG. Soldiers in the secondary zone may be boarded with 45 months TIS.

In addition to TIG and TIS, each soldier promoted to staff sergeant:

- must be recommended by a promotion selection board

- must have a minimum of 12 months Active Federal Service remaining at the time of promotion

- must be a graduate of the PLDC prior to being recommended for promotion

- must be a graduate of the BNCOC, effective October 1, 1992

- must possess either a high school diploma, GED equivalency, or an associate or higher degree.

The minimum promotion point score for attaining recommended list status for promotion to staff sergeant (E-6) is 550 points (Table 2.3).

Centralized Promotions

Prior to centralization, soldiers could not compete for promotion unless a position/grade vacancy existed at the unit of assignment. These requirements did not allow for equitable promotion opportunities for all soldiers. On January 1, 1969, March 1, 1969, and June 1, 1970, promotions to sergeant major (E-9), master sergeant (E-8), and sergeant first class (E-7) were centralized at HQDA.

Senior enlisted promotions are announced monthly by MOS. The number of soldiers to be promoted each month is determined by the Office of the Deputy Chief of Staff for Personnel (ODCSPER) in coordination with the Director, Enlisted Personnel Management, PERSCOM, and are based on requirements for individual MOS, rank, and budgetary constraints.

The promotion board consists of at least five members, and unlike the procedures of the promotion boards governing promotions to E-5 and E-6, the soldier does not appear before the board. The soldier is considered for promotion using the "whole soldier" concept, whereby the soldier's qualifications for promotion are based on his or her entire record. The promotion board's analysis of the soldier's file includes an evaluation of the scope and variety of assignments; an estimate of potential expected of an NCO at the next higher grade; trends of efficiency; the length of service and maturity; awards, decorations, and commendations; education (military and civilian[4]); moral standards, integrity, and character; and general physical condition.

---

[4]The military educational requirement for advancement to E-7 is the completion of the Advanced Noncommissioned Officers' Course (ANCOC).

3. Navy Enlisted Promotion

The Navy Enlisted Advancement System (NEAS) "provides for the orderly progression of qualified enlisted personnel to higher levels of responsibility throughout their naval careers." (BUPERSINST 1430.16D.)

The NEAS is based on naval standards (NAVSTDs) and occupational standards (OCCSTDs). NAVSTDs are the military requirements of all Navy enlisted personnel and the minimum performance requirements within a rate and rating, while OCCSTDs are the minimum enlisted occupational skills. NEAS evaluates the "whole person" and promotes the best-qualified candidates based on a point system[1] combining three main factors: examination, performance, and experience. Specifically, points are received for exam score, performance factors, length of service, service in paygrade, and awards; however, the most significant requirement is the recommendation of the commanding officer.

Advancement in rate or change in rating is based on demonstrated proficiency in assigned duties and on a written exam. In the Navy, rate, instead of rank, defines personnel by paygrade and a general rating identifies a broad occupational field.[2]

Tables 3.1 and 3.2 present the time-in-rate (TIR) requirements and target advancement, and the Total Active Federal Military Service (TAFMS) (time-in-service) requirements for promotion. TIR dates are established for each individual on initial entry into the Navy, on reentry, and on advancement or reduction in rate.

---

[1]Final multiple score (FMS).

[2]Certain general ratings are subdivided into service ratings that provide for increased specialization in training and employment of personnel.

Table 3.1

TIR Requirements and Target Advancement, Navy

Paygrade	Service Requirements	Target Advancement
E-1 to E-2	9 months in paygrade E-1	9 months
E-2 to E-3	9 months in paygrade E-2	18 months
E-3 to E-4	6 months in paygrade E-3	2 years
E-4 to E-5	12 months in paygrade E-4	3 years
E-5 to E-6	36 months in paygrade E-5	6 years
E-6 to E-7	36 months in paygrade E-6	9 years
E-7 to E-8	36 months in paygrade E-7	12 years
E-8 to E-9	36 months in paygrade E-8	15 years

SOURCE: BUPERSINST 1430.16D, 1991.

Advancement to General Apprenticeship, Apprentice (E-2), and General Apprenticeship (E-3)

Advancement to general apprenticeship, apprentice (E-2), and general apprenticeship (E-3) is based on time-in-rate and a recommendation from the chain of command. Commanding officers may advance qualified personnel without numerical limitations. Apprenticeship examinations are not required for advancement to E-2, and, although examination is required for advancement to E-3, the individual only needs to pass. The examination consists of 150 questions with 100 questions addressing the individual's specific apprenticeship and 50 questions covering naval standards and general military subjects.

Advancement to Petty Officer, Third Class (E-4), Through Chief Petty Officer (E-7)

Although there are no limits on the number of advancements to paygrades E-2 and E-3, there is a limit on the number of advancements per fiscal year to paygrades E-4 through E-7.[3] General eligibility requirements include TIR (Table 3.1), personnel advancement requirements (PARs), and performance tests.

PARs are mandatory for advancement to paygrades E-4 through E-7[4] and should be completed before commands make a recommendation for advancement. PARs, demonstrated by performance, are checklists of the minimum occupational skills and abilities required for advancement or change in rating.

---

[3]BUPERS determines vacancies based on current and prospective losses, and the CNO specifies the number of advancements per month within each paygrade and class of service based on the vacancies.

[4]PARs are not required for advancement to paygrades E-2, E-3, E-8, or E-9.

Table 3.2

**Total Active Federal Military Service
Requirements, Navy**

Paygrade	Department of Defense TAFMS
E-2	6 months
E-3	1 year
E-4	2 years
E-5	3 years
E-6	7 years
E-7	11 years
E-8	16 years
E-9	19 years

SOURCE: BUPERSINST 1430.16D, 1991.

PARs are noncompetitive and a relative or absolute grade is not assigned. Each PAR item is a statement of a rating-required occupational ability and is used as an evaluation guide. Each individual is evaluated on the ability to satisfactorily perform the PAR, and the evaluation is based on an actual demonstration of the PAR. Three examples of the approximately 100 PARs for an aviation machinist's mate (AD) are (1) perform maintenance on power plant engine intake system components, (2) perform maintenance on engine electrical systems, and (3) clean/lubricate engine power control systems.

Table 3.3 shows how the FMS computation for petty officer, third class (E-4), through chief petty officer (E-7) is computed. The FMS computation is based on six factors: a standard score (SS)[5] on a Navywide Advancement-in-Rate Examination, performance factor, length of service, service in paygrade, awards, and pass-not-advanced (PNA) points. The total maximum score for promotion to E-4 and E-5 is 230 points and 264 points for promotion to E-6. The maximum score for promotion to E-7 is 132 points based only on a standard score and performance factors. The FMS results for all candidates are rank-ordered from the most qualified to the least qualified. The number of quotas available determines the number of selectees for advancement.

The standard score is based on a Navywide advancement examination normally administered[6] semiannually in March and September for advancement to E-4 through E-6 and annually in January for advancement to E-7. Candidates taking the exam in March or September are advanced beginning in July or January, respectively. Candidates who take the exam and are selected for advancement

---

[5]The standard score, not raw score, is the component of the FMS.

[6]Generally, 135 questions pertain to the rating and 15 questions pertain to general military subjects.

but are not advanced in the initial cut are promoted in increments, usually monthly, through the months prior to the next exam cycle (Table 3.4). E-7 candidates are designated "selection board eligible" if their FMS is in the top 60 percent of their rating. Personnel selected for advancement by the selection board are then advanced in increments starting the September following the exam. They are also advanced in increments through the next year based on the number of slots open in their rating. Petty officer examinations consist of 150 questions.

The performance factor is calculated using a performance mark average (PMA), i.e., the average of the current paygrade's evaluation(s). The minimum PMA for advancement is 2.6 for E-4 through E-6 and 3.0 for E-7. Candidates who pass the exam but are not selected for advancement may receive PNA points toward the next advancement exam cycle. PNA points are calculated in fractions of one-half point to a maximum of 1.5 points in each of two categories (test score and PMA). Total PNA points are earned from the most recent five exams of the last six exam cycles. Candidates' PNA points are comparable against the relative standing of their counterparts (Table 3.5).

Advancement to Senior Chief Petty Officer and Master Chief Petty Officer

Promotions to senior chief petty officer (E-8) and master chief petty officer (E-9) do not require examinations. However, commanding officer's recommendation is required as well as selection board action. Recommendations for advancement to E-8 and E-9 are normally submitted annually in November.

Each candidate for advancement receives two reviews from two different panel members of the board. A third reviewer examines the record if there is a significant difference in the first two reviews. The board reviews the Enlisted Summary Record (ESR) of each candidate. The ESR contains information on the candidate's exam rate, TIR, TIS, history of assignments, education, evaluation history, and various other data elements extracted from the enlisted master file (EMF) and the inactive enlisted master file (IEMF).

Additional factors considered by the board include professional performance at sea, improving educational level, career history, potential, and, most important, sustained superior performance.

12

Table 3.3

FMS Computation for E-4 Through E-7 Exams, Navy

Factor	Exam Paygrade	Computation	E-4/E-5 Exam Max Points (%)	E-6 Exam Max Points (%)	E-7 Exam Max Points (%)
Standard Score	All		80 (35%)	80 (30%)	80 (60%)
Performance Factor	E-4/E-5	(PMA[a] x 50) − 130	70 (30%)		
	E-6	(PMA x 50) − 108		92 (35%)	
	E-7	(PMA x 13)			52 (40%)
Length of Service	E-4/E-5	(TAS[b] − SIPG[c]) + 15	30 (13%)	34 (13%)	
	E-6	(TAS − SIPG) + 15			
Service in Paygrade	E-4/E-5	(2 x SIPG) + 15	30 (13%)	34 (13%)	
(7.5 years max SIPG)	E-6	(2 x SIPG) + 19			
Awards	E-4/E-5	Varies depending on award	10 (4.5%)	12 (4.5%)	
	E-6				
PNA[d] Points	E-4/E-5		10 (4.5%)	12 (4.5%)	
	E-6				
Total Points			230 (100%)	264 (100%)	132 (100%)

[a]Performance Mark Average; the maximum PMA a candidate can achieve is 4.00.
[b]Total Active Service.
[c]Service in Paygrade.
[d]Passed Not Advanced.
SOURCE: BUPERSINST 1430.16D, 1991.

Table 3.4

Advancement Schedule for Promotion to E-4 Through E-9

Candidates for Promotion to	Exam or Nomination	Selection Board Convenes	Selectees Notified	Advancement Increments/ Segments
E-4/E-5/E-6	March	NA	June	July–December
	September	NA	November	January–June
E-7	January	June	August	September– August
E-8/E-9	November[a]	March	June	July–June

[a]Month of nomination for advancement by commanding officer.
SOURCE: BUPERSINST 1430.16D, 1991.

Table 3.5

Crediting PNA Points

Member's Relative Points Test Score	PNA Points Credited	Candidate's Relative Performance Mark Average	PNA Points Credited
Top 25 percent	1.5	Top 25 percent	1.5
Next 25 percent	1.0	Next 25 percent	1.0
Next 25 percent	0.5	Next 25 percent	0.5

SOURCE: BUPERSINST 1430.16D, p. 8-6.

4. Marine Corps Enlisted Promotion

The U.S. Marine Corps enlisted promotion basic policy states that "all promotions must positively contribute to the high standards of leadership and proficiency required for continued combat readiness." There are two objectives of the enlisted promotion system: "maintain the actual strength in each grade and military occupational specialty (MOS) at the maximum readiness for commitment to combat;" and "insure that all eligible Marines receive full and equitable opportunity to compete for promotion." (MCO P1400.32B.)

Enlisted Marines within each grade and MOS or occupational field (OccFld) compete among themselves for promotion to the next higher grade.

Promotion to Private First Class (E-2) and Lance Corporal (E-3)

There are no point requirements for promotions up to grade of lance corporal. Given that Marine service has been satisfactory, Marines who have served for six months on active duty in the grade of private (E-1) will be promoted to private first class (E-2). Similarly, Marines in grade E-2 who have eight months TIG and nine months TIS may be promoted to lance corporal (E-3) (Table 4.1). Promotion to lance corporal further requires the commanding officer to determine qualification for promotion. The Marine Corps Total Force System (MCTFS) automatically identifies eligible personnel for promotion, and identification occurs the month prior to the promotion month. Promotions occur on the first day of the promotion month.

Promotion to Corporal (E-4) and Sergeant (E-5)

Promotions to the grade of corporal and sergeant are authorized on the basis of vacancies existing throughout the Marine Corps and are effected by authorized commanders. Promotions vary monthly by primary MOS and are based on automatic composite scores (CS), which are computed quarterly for each eligible lance corporal. The CS is a mathematical evaluation used as a Marine Corps–wide comparison of Marines within a given grade and MOS.

Table 4.1

Minimum TIG and TIS Requirements, Marine Corps

Promotion to		Regular Promotion		Merit Promotion	
		TIG	TIS	TIG	TIS
E-2	PFC	6 months	6 months	NA	none
E-3	LCpl	8 months	9 months	NA	none
E-4	Cpl	8 months	12 months	NA	6 months
E-5	Sgt	12 months	24 months	NA	18 months
E-6	SSgt	27 months	4 years	NA	4 years
E-7	GySgt	3 years	6 years	NA	6 years
E-8	1stSgt/MSgt	4 years	8 years	—	—
E-9	SgtMaj/MGySgt	3 years	10 years	—	—

SOURCE: MCO P1400.32.B, 1996.

Advancement to corporal and sergeant requires a CS[1] equal to or above the established cut score[2] and minimum TIG and TIS requirements (Table 4.1). Promotions to corporal and sergeant are effected once per quarter for each MOS.

Computation of CS

Table 4.2 shows the rating system used in the automated computation of CSs for lance corporals and corporals. The CS is based on a variety of performance factors: rifle marksmanship, physical fitness, duty performance, conduct, and education.

Rifle marksmanship is tested once a year during an annual qualification period. Scores received are converted into ratings for calculation of the CS. For example, the maximum score of 250 converts into a rating of 5.0.

Like the rifle marksmanship score, the physical fitness test (PFT) score is also converted into a rating. However, both age and gender influence the rating received. There are four age and gender groups: men between the ages of 17 and 26, men 27 and older, women between the ages of 17 and 26, and women 27 and older. The maximum PFT score is 300. For scores down to 225, a rating of 4.4 is received regardless of gender or age. However, lower PFT scores are converted differently for each age and gender group. For example, a PFT score of 150 for a man between the ages of 17 and 26 is converted to a 3.0 rating and 3.6 for a man 27 or older. A woman between the ages of 17 and 26 scoring 150 on the PFT receives a rating one full point higher than her male counterparts, 4.0; however, a woman 27-years-old or older receives the same score as a male in the

---

[1]CSs remain in effect for three months, which is equal to one promotion quarter.
[2]Cut scores are computed monthly for each MOS.

same age group, 3.6. Furthermore, the lowest PFT score to receive a rating is different for each age and gender group. The lowest score for men between 17 and 26 is 135 with a rating of 3.0; however, men 27 and older can receive a score 25 points lower, 110, and receive the same rating, 3.0. The lowest PFT score for women between 17 and 26 is 100 with a rating of 3.0, and the lowest PFT score for women 27 and older is 73 with a rating of 3.6.

Average duty proficiency is determined by a commander, through interview, observation, proficiency marks received in lower grades, or any combination of the above. All duty proficiency marks assigned and all conduct marks assigned are averaged and multiplied by 100.

The drill instructor (DI)/recruiter/Marine security guard (MSG) bonus of 100 points applies to lance corporals and corporals who have satisfactory performance in the following categories:

- DIs in the grade of corporal

- Corporals assigned as recruiters

- MSGs in the grades of lance corporal and corporal.

Self-education bonus applies only to courses completed since last promotion or reduction. Bonus points range from 1.0 to 1.5 points per completed approved course. Approved courses include the Marine Corps Instruction (MCI) course or other military service correspondence course, extension school subcourse, College Level Examination Program (CLEP) test, and college and vocational school courses.

The command recruiting bonus applies to participation in the command recruiting program. Twenty bonus points are awarded for each individual referred. A maximum of 100 bonus points may be awarded.

Noncommissioned Officer Promotions

Selection boards convene once a calendar year to examine qualifications of Marines in the grades of sergeant (E-5), staff sergeant (E-6), gunnery sergeant (E-7), master sergeant (E-8), and first sergeant (E-8) and recommend those best equipped for promotion to the next higher grade. Selection board membership generally consists of 16 to 18 members. The board's evaluation and consideration of each Marine's qualifications are measured by the "best fitted" concept, which encompasses achievement, leadership, experience (types and levels), professional and technical knowledge, growth potential, motivation,

Table 4.2

CS Computation Form

Line No.		Rating Score
1.	Rifle Marksmanship Score _____ =	_____
2.	Physical Fitness Test Score _____ =	_____
3.	Subtotal (line 1 + 2)	_____
4.	GMP Score (line 3 divided by _____)[a]	_____
5.	GMP Score (from line 4) ____ x 100	_____
6.	Average Duty Proficiency ____ x 100	_____
7.	Average Conduct ____ x 100	_____
8.	TIG (months) _____ x 5	_____
9.	TIS (months) _____ x 2	_____
10.	DI/Recruiter/MSG Bonus _____ x 1	_____
11.	Self-Education Bonus:	
	a. MCI/Extension School _____	
	b. College/CLEP/Vocational _____ (a) + (b)	
	x 10 =	_____
12.	Command Recruiting Bonus _____ x 1	_____
13.	Composite Score (sum of lines 5 through 12)	_____

[a]The General Military Proficiency (GMP) score is calculated by dividing line three by the number of lines that have a rating other than NC—"not considered." The number used to divide the subtotal (line 3) will be either one or two.
SOURCE: Marine Corps Order P1400.32B, Chapter 2.

general military proficiency, personal appearance, special qualifications (e.g., language skills), physical condition, moral character, and maturity.

Promotion to First Sergeant (E-8) and Sergeant Major (E-9)

The first sergeants and sergeant majors are the principal enlisted assistants to the commanding officers of the commands to which they are assigned. Outstanding leadership is the primary and foremost requisite for promotion. The board also considers the candidate's degree of professional competence in troop leadership and the ability in all administrative, technical, and tactical requirements of the organization.

All gunnery sergeants (E-7) who meet the TIG and TIS requirements are eligible to compete for first sergeant (Table 4.1). Gunnery sergeants indicate their preference for promotion to first sergeant or master sergeant on their fitness report.[3]

In addition to TIG and TIS requirements, candidates for promotion must

---

[3]The sergeant major will be selected only from eligible first sergeants; master gunnery sergeants will be selected only from eligible master sergeants.

- exhibit strong ability to read and interpret regulations, communicate verbally and in writing, and be able to research all matters affecting personnel

- have exhibited a consistent and exemplary standard of military appearance, physical fitness, and personal discipline

- have completed the SNCO Academy Career and Advanced courses

- have demonstrated ability to lead groups of Marines of at least squad size

- have demonstrated ability to function in an independent environment or have successfully completed a tour in a "B" billet (e.g., DI, MSG, or recruiting)

- must be serving on active duty on the date the appropriate regular selection board convenes.

Promotion to Master Sergeant (E-8) and Master Gunnery Sergeant (E-9)

The master sergeants and master gunnery sergeants are the technical leaders of their fields. The primary requisite for advancement to master sergeant or master gunnery sergeant is outstanding proficiency in the assigned occupational field. Additionally, an exceptionally high degree of leadership and supervisory ability and the ability to act independently as enlisted assistants in all administrative, technical, and tactical requirements of their occupational specialty are necessary for advancement.

Gunnery sergeants who meet the TIG and TIS requirements (Table 4.1) will receive consideration for master sergeant, without regard to the preference for first sergeant or master sergeant as indicated on the fitness report.

5. Air Force Enlisted Promotion

The Air Force promotes airmen and noncommissioned officers (NCOs) who show potential for more responsibility through an objective and visible centralized[1] promotion system. Furthermore, the Air Force promotes airmen to fill particular needs for specific grades in each Air Force Specialty Code (AFSC).

The Department of Defense sets limits, related to fiscal year–end strength, on the number of airmen allowed in the top five grades (E-5 through E-9). In addition to being affected by funding and regulatory limits, promotion quotas are also affected by the number of projected vacancies in specific grades. Public law limits the number of airmen who may serve on active duty in grades of senior master sergeant (E-8) and chief master sergeant (E-9) to 3 percent of the enlisted force with no more that 1 percent serving in E-9.[2]

The Air Force enlisted promotion system is based primarily on sufficient TIG, sufficient TIS, skill level, a point system, and a recommendation by the immediate commander.

There are five different skill levels within an Air Force Specialty (AFS). The first skill level, 1-skill level (helper), identifies personnel classified in an AFS when entering the Air Force or when retraining. The second skill level, 3-skill level (apprentice), identifies airmen who have obtained basic knowledge within an AFSC but who require supervision to perform job tasks because of the lack of experience and proficiency. The third level of skill, 5-skill level (journeyman), identifies airmen who have shown proficiency through experience and training. Airmen with 5-skill level can be expected to perform on the job without direct supervision.[3] The fourth skill level, 7-skill level (craftsman), identifies airmen who have gained a high degree of technical knowledge in the AFS and who have acquired supervisory capability through training and experience. The fifth level, 9-skill level (superintendent), identifies airmen who, through experience, training, and performance, have shown management and supervisory ability to fill positions requiring broad general knowledge.

---

[1] Except for promotion through senior airman (E-4), the promotion system is centralized.

[2] This limit also applies to the Army, Marine Corps, and Navy. (Title 10 U.S.C. 517.)

[3] In specialties where a 5-skill level does not exist, personnel are considered skilled at the 3-skill level.

For airmen to qualify for skill level upgrading, they must satisfy three specific requirements: career knowledge, job proficiency, and job experience. On-the-job training (OJT) programs satisfy the requirements for career knowledge and job proficiency. Job experience is measured by satisfactorily performing tasks over a minimum specified time period. Table 5.1 lists the criteria for awarding airmen AFSCs, Special Duty Identifiers (SDIs), or Chief Enlisted Manager (CEM) codes.

Table 5.2 lists the minimum eligibility requirements for promotion, including skill levels. Table 5.3 presents TIS and TIG requirements, promotion eligibility cutoff dates (PECDs), and test cycles for promotion to airman (E-2) through chief master sergeant (E-9) that ensure timely periodic promotions and accurate forecasting of vacancies.

Table 5.1

Criteria for Awarding Airmen AFSCs, SDIs, or CEM Codes, Air Force

	If the airman	then the airman is qualified for award of AFSC, SDI, or CEM code as indicated
1	is assigned permanent duty or training in a helper AFSC and meets specialty entry qualifications for the AFS	1-skill level.
2	completes an AFSC awarding course	3-skill level.
3	satisfactorily completes three-month apprenticeship period, successfully completes mandatory Career Development Courses (CDCs), completes all core tasks identified in the Career Field Education and Training Plan (CFETP) and other duty position tasks identified by the individual's instructor, completes 15 months in upgrade training, meets mandatory 5-skill level requirements	5-skill level.
4	satisfactorily completes all mandatory 7-skill level training, is a SSgt (E-5) or above, and is recommended by a supervisor, completes 18 months OJT, meets all mandatory 7-skill level requirements	7-skill level.
5	is satisfactorily performing in an AFSC, is a SMSgt (E-8), possesses a 7-skill level AFSC, which is normal input source into 9-skill level AFSC, completes all training requirements, completes the Senior NCO Academy (in-residence or by correspondence), is recommended by supervisor, and meets mandatory 9-skill level requirements	9-skill level.
6	is a CMSgt or CMSgt select and has 9-skill level feeder AFSC that is normal input source into CEM code	CEM code.
7	is approved for duty in an SDI or Reporting Identifier (RI)	SDI or RI.

SOURCE: Air Force Instruction 36-2101, 1 May 1998.

Table 5.2

Minimum Eligibility Requirements for Promotion, Air Force

If promotion is to the grade of	and the PAFSC as of PECD is at the	and time in current grade on the first day of the month before the month promotions are normally made in the cycle is	and the TAFMS on the first day of the last month of the promotion cycle is	and the member has	then
SrA	3-level	NA	1 year[a]		the airman is eligible for promotion if recommended in writing by the promotion authority. The individual must serve on active duty in enlisted status as of the PECD and serve in continuous active duty until the effective date of promotion.
SSgt	5-level	6 months	3 years		
TSgt	7-level	23 months	5 years		
MSgt	7-level	24 months	8 years	8 years cumulative enlisted service creditable for basic pay	
SMSgt	7-level	20 months	11 years		
CMSgt	9-level	21 months	14 years	10 years cumulative enlisted service creditable for basic pay	

[a]Must have 36 months TIS and 20 months TIG, or 28 months TIG, whichever comes first.

PAFSC = Primary Air Force Specialty Code.

PECD = Promotion eligibility cutoff date.

TAFMS = Total Active Federal Military Service.

SOURCE: Air Force Pamphlet 36-2241, Volume 1, 1 July 1995.

Promotion to Airman (E-2) and Airman First Class (E-3)

Airmen with a recommendation from their commander are eligible for
promotion and are normally promoted on a noncompetitive basis. The TIG
requirement for an airman basic to be eligible for promotion is six months and 10
months for an airman first class (Table 5.3).

Promotion to Senior Airman (E-4)

As indicated in Table 5.3, the Air Force promotes airmen first class (E-3) to senior
airmen (E-4) with either 36 months TIS and 20 months TIG, or 28 months TIG,
whichever occurs first. In addition to TIG and TIS requirements, E-3s must be
recommended by their unit commander and must have a 3-skill level to be
eligible for promotion.[4]

Promotion to Staff Sergeant (E-5), Technical Sergeant (E-6), and Master Sergeant (E-7)

Promotions to E-5 through E-7 occur under one of two programs: the Weighted
Airman Promotion System (WAPS) or Stripes for Exceptional Performers (STEP).

Table 5.3

**TIS and TIG Requirements, PECDs, Test Cycles for Promotion,
and High Year of Tenure for Airman Through Chief
Master Sergeant, Air Force**

	TIS	TIG	PECD	Test Cycle
E-2	—	6 months	NA	NA
E-3	—	10 months	NA	NA
E-4[a]	36 months	20 months or 28 months	NA	NA
E-5	3 years	6 months	31 March	April-June
E-6	5 years	23 months	31 December	January-March
E-7	8 years	24 months	31 December	January-March
E-8	11 years	20 months	30 September	October
E-9	14 years	21 months	31 July	August

[a]Must have either 36 months TIS and 20 months TIG, or 28 months
TIG, whichever comes first.
SOURCE: Air Force Pamphlet 36-2241, Volume 1, 1 July 1995.

---

[4]Airmen must meet skill level requirements by the effective date of promotion for E-4.

Individual must meet minimum TIS, TIG, skill level[5] requirements, and PECDs listed in Tables 5.2 and 5.3.

Weighted Airman Promotion System (WAPS)

In a process initiated in 1970, the Air Force replaced a subjective promotion board system with the WAPS. Table 5.4 lists the six clearly defined weighted factors that make up WAPS: Specialty Knowledge Test (SKT), Promotion Fitness Examination (PFE), TIS, TIG, decorations,[6] and performance reports. The assigned points are based on the factor's importance relative to promotion. The total number of points possible under WAPS is 460 with more than 40 percent of the score accounted by the SKT and PFE.

SKT is a 100-point multiple-choice test that measures career field knowledge.[7] The PFE, also a 100-question multiple-choice test, measures knowledge of military subjects and management practices at a specific grade level. Specifically, questions focus on the mission, organization, and history of the Air Force; evolution of the enlisted force; career NCO; entitlements and benefits; customs and courtesies; standards of conduct; individual rights; appearance standards; enforcing standards; leadership; communication; counseling; quality; human resources; resource management and the environment; security; and safety and survival. The amount of knowledge required of each topic depends on grade level. Three levels of understanding determine the difficulty of the questions:

Table 5.4

WAPS for Grades Staff Sergeant Through Master Sergeant, Air Force

Factors	Weights
SKT	100
PFE	100
TIS	40
TIG	60
Decorations	25
EPRs and APRs	135
Total	460

SOURCE: Air Force Instruction 36-2502, 1994.

---

[5] Airmen must meet skill-level requirements by the PECD for E-5. E-5s can test and compete for promotion to E-6 if they have a 5-skill level as of PECD; however, they must have a 7-skill level before promotion.

[6] A listing of decorations and corresponding points is in Appendix B.

[7] For those individuals exempt from SKT, the PFE score is doubled.

knowledge (K), comprehension (C), and application (A). Questions coded A are more difficult than questions coded C. For most topics, requirement understanding is the same for promotion to staff sergeant through chief master sergeant (E-5 through E-9). For example, the required knowledge of the code of conduct for promotion to staff sergeant (E-5) through chief master sergeant (E-9) is comprehension. However, a few topics require greater understanding for advancement to higher ranks. For instance, understanding of manpower management for advancement to staff sergeant and technical sergeant (E-6) requires comprehension, while advancement to master sergeant (E-7) through chief master sergeant requires application.

The Enlisted Performance Report (EPR) score accounts for more than one-quarter of the total WAPS score and is an evaluation of behavior, performance, achievement, and efficiency.

Seven questions evaluating performance are on the EPR for airman basic (E-1) through technical sergeant (E-6) (AF Form 910). These questions address topics regarding conduct, performance and knowledge of duties, communication skills, supervisory and leadership abilities, and compliance with standards and training requirements. Raters[8] group performance into one of four levels. For example, for the question that inquires how well the ratee performs assigned duties—considering quantity, quality, and timeliness of duties performed—the rater places the ratee in one of four categories: (1) inefficient, an unprofessional performer; (2) good performer, performs routine duties satisfactorily; (3) excellent performer, consistently produces high-quality work; and (4) the exception, absolutely superior in all areas.

On the senior EPR for master sergeant (E-7) through chief master sergeant (E-9) (AF Form 911), performance is also evaluated with seven questions. The questions address duty performance, job knowledge, leadership, managerial skills, judgment, professional qualities, and communication skills. Performance is grouped into one of four levels. For example, for the question that addresses judgment, considering how well the ratee evaluates situations and reaches logical conclusions, the rater places the ratee in one of four categories: (1) poor; (2) sound; (3) emphasizes logic and decisionmaking; and (4) highly respected and skilled. (Copies of AF Forms 910 and 911 are in Appendix D.)

---

[8]The rater is usually the ratee's immediate supervisor. A rater is an officer or NCO of a U.S. or foreign military service in a grade equal to or higher than the ratee, or a civilian (GS-5, a comparable grade, or higher) in a supervisory position higher than the ratee in the ratee's rating chain (AFI 36-2403).

There are at least two evaluators for all AF Forms 910 and 911, and commanders review all EPRs. Performance and promotion potential is scored with one of five recommendations: not recommend, not recommend at this time, consider, ready, and immediate promotion. Each EPR rating within the last five years with a maximum of 10 ratings is used to compute the EPR score. Each report rating is weighted by time, with more recent reports receiving more weight.

Stripes for Exceptional Performers (STEP)

Instituted in 1980, the STEP program allows for unique circumstances that clearly justify promotion, in the commander's judgment. Commanders of Major Commands (MAJCOMs), Field Operating Agencies (FOAs), and senior officers of organizations with large enlisted populations may promote a limited number of airmen with exceptional potential to grades of staff sergeant through master sergeant (E-5 through E-7).

Under STEP, at least three years of TIS and completion of the Airman Leadership School are requirements for promotions to staff sergeant. Five years of TIS is required for promotions to technical sergeant (E-6). Eight years of TIS and completion of the in-resident Noncommissioned Officer Academy are required for promotions to master sergeant (E-7).

Promotion to Senior Master Sergeant (E-8) and Chief Master Sergeant (E-9)

Consideration for promotion to senior master sergeant and chief master sergeant is a two-phase process consisting of WAPS factors and a central evaluation board using the whole-person concept at Headquarters, Air Force Military Personnel Center (HQAFMPC). Table 5.5 lists the WAPS weighted factors for promotions

Table 5.5

WAPS for Senior Master Sergeant and Chief Master Sergeant

Factors	Weights
USAF Supervisory Exam	100
EPR	135
Professional Military Education	15
Decorations	25
TIG	60
TIS	25
Total	360

SOURCE: Air Force Instruction 36-2502, 1994.

to E-8 and E-9. The WAPS factors differ slightly from those used for promotion eligibility of staff sergeant through master sergeant. For example, the total number of possible points is 360 for E-8 and E-9 and 460 points for E-5 through E-7. The central evaluation board's subjective evaluation uses the individual's record and scores range from 270 to 450 points. Thus, these two phases are worth up to 810 total points total.

Appendix

A. Paygrade, General Title, and Abbreviations

Table A.1

Paygrade, General Title, and Abbreviations Across Services

Pay-grade		Army		Navy		Marine Corps		Air Force
E-1	PV1	Private E-1		General Apprenticeship, Recruit	Pvt	Private	AB	Airman Basic
E-2	PV2	Private E-2		General Apprenticeship, Apprentice		Private First Class	Amn	Airman
E-3	PFC	Private First Class		General Apprenticeship	LCpl	Lance Corporal	A1C	Airman First Class
E-4	SPC	Specialist	PO3	Petty Officer, 3rd Class	Cpl	Corporal	SrA	Senior Airman
E-5	SGT	Sergeant	PO2	Petty Officer, 2nd Class	Sgt	Sergeant	SSgt	Staff Sergeant
E-6	SSG	Staff Sergeant	PO1	Petty Officer, 1st Class	SSgt	Staff Sergeant	TSgt	Technical Sergeant
E-7	SFC	Sergeant First Class	CPO	Chief Petty Officer	GySgt	Gunnery Sergeant	MSgt	Master Sergeant
E-8	MSG	Master Sergeant	SPO	Senior Chief Petty Officer	MSgt / 1stSgt	Master Sergeant / First Sergeant	SMSgt	Senior Master Sergeant
E-9	SGM	Sergeant Major	MCPO	Master Chief Petty Officer	MGySst	Master Gunnery Sergeant	CMSgt	Chief Master Sergeant
					SgtMaj	Sergeant Major		

B. Award and Decoration Points

Table B.1

Army Award and Decoration Points

Decoration	Value
Soldier's Medal or higher award	35
Bronze Star Medal (Valor or Merit)	30
Purple Heart	30
Defense Meritorious Service Medal	25
Meritorious Service Medal	25
Air Medal (Valor or Merit)	20
Joint Service Commendation Medal	20
Army Commendation Medal (Valor or Merit)	20
Joint Service Achievement Medal	15
Combat Infantry Badge	15
Combat Field Medical Badge	15
Army Achievement Medal	10
Army Reserve Component Achievement Medal	10
Good Conduct Medal	10
Expert Infantry Badge	10
Basic U.S. Army Recruiter Badge (each subsequent award, that is Gold Achievement Star, Gold Recruiter Badge, Sapphire Achievement Star, will receive 5 points)	10
Ranger Tab	10
Parachutist Badge	5
Parachute Rigger Badge	5
Divers Badge	5
Explosive Ordnance Disposal Badge	5
Pathfinder Badge	5
Aircraft Crewman Badge	5
Nuclear Reactor Badge	5
Special Forces Tab	5
Driver and Mechanic Badge (maximum 5 points)	5
Air Assault Badge	5
Drill Sergeant Identification Badge	5
Campaign Star (Battle Star)	5
Tomb Guard Identification Badge	5

SOURCE: Army Regulation 600-8-19, 1 November 1991 with Interim Change I01, 8 April 1994.

Table B.2

Navy Award and Decoration Points

Award	Points
Medal of Honor	10
Distinguished Service Medal or Cross	4
Silver Star	4
Legion of Merit	4
Distinguished Flying Cross	4
Navy and Marine Corps Medal	3
Soldier's Medal	3
Bronze Star Medal	3
Purple Heart	3
Defense Meritorious Service Medal	3
Meritorious Service Medal	3
Gold Life Saving Medal	3
Joint Service Commendation Medal	3
Commendation Medal	3
Letter of Commendation (addressed personally to the individual from the President, Secretary of Defense and Secretary of any U.S. military service, or military heads of any U.S. military service	2
Joint Service Achievement Medal	2
Achievement Medal	2
Combat Action Ribbon	2
Navy Good Conduct Medal	2
	(Max 10)
Enlisted Aviation Warfare Insignia	2
Enlisted Surface Warfare Insignia	2
Enlisted Special Warfare Insignia	2
Submarine Qualification Insignia (Dolphins)	2
Aviation Aircrew Insignia (Aircrew Wings)	2
Basic or Senior Master Explosive Ordnance Disposal Badge (NEC 5332/3/4/5)	2
Bachelor's Degree (or above)	2[a]
Naval Reserve Meritorious Service Medal	1
	(Max 10)
Air Medal (Strike/Flight)	1
	(Max 5)
Type 4/8 Overseas Duty	1
Persian Gulf MSO Double Tour/Patrol Boats	1
Letter of Commendation signed by flag officer	1
	(Max 2)[b]
Associate's Degree	1
Recruiter Duty	1

SOURCE: BUPERSINST 1430.16D, pp. 4-9–4-12.

   [a]One point may be assigned for an associate's degree and two points for baccalaureate (or above) degree. The maximum award for educational achievement is two points.

   [b]A letter of commendation signed by a flag officer will be credited to the awards factor for E-4, E-5, and E-6 candidates only.

Table B.3

Air Force Decoration Points

Decoration	Value
Medal of Honor	15
Air Force Distinguished Cross	11
Navy Distinguished Cross	11
Defense Distinguished Service Medal	9
Distinguished Service Medal	9
Silver Star	9
Legion of Merit	7
Defense Superior Service Medal	7
Distinguished Flying Cross	7
Airman's/Soldier's/Navy-Marine Corps/Coast Guard/Bronze Star/Defense Meritorious Service Medals	5
Purple Heart	5
Air/Aerial Achievement	3
Air Force Commendation Medal	3
Army Commendation Medal	3
Navy Commendation Medal	3
Joint Services Commendation Medal	3
Coast Guard Commendation Medal	3
Air Force Achievement Medal	1
Navy Achievement Medal	1
Coast Guard Achievement Medal	1

Source: Air Force Instruction 36-2502, 1994.

C. Army Promotion Point Worksheet

PROMOTION POINT WORKSHEET	1. TYPE	2. DATE
For use of this form, see AR 600-8-19; the proponent agency is ODCSPER	☐ a. Initial ☐ b. Reevaluation ☐ c. Recomputation	

DATA REQUIRED BY THE PRIVACY ACT OF 1974

AUTHORITY: Title 5 USC, Section 301.

PRINCIPAL PURPOSE: To determine eligibilty for promotion.

ROUTINE USES: Information may be referred to appropriate authorities to determine promotion eligibility and validity of points granted.

DISCLOSURE: Voluntary failure to furnish information requested may result in denial of promotion.

3. NAME	4. SSN	5. GRADE
6. CURRENT ORGANIZATION	7. SRB MOS 8. PMOS 9. RECOMMENDED GRADE/CPMOS	

SECTION A - RECOMMENDATION

10. FROM (Commander)	11. THROUGH (Promotion Authority)	12. TO (PSC)

13. Under the provisions of AR 600-8-19, chapter 3 (Active Army); AR 140-158, chapter 3 (USAR); or NGR 600-200, chapter 6 (ARNG) (check one of the following):

a. Recommend the above-named soldier for promotion/reevaluation to the grade indicated. (Complete lines 13b (1) - (6) and send to the promotion authority.)

b. Request the following information be used in the next scheduled recomputation of promotion points. (Complete lines 13(b)(2) - (6) and send to the PSC.)

(1) Waivers required (maximum of two allowed)	(2) Most recent individual assigned weapon qualification	
(a) Time in Service	(a) Expert	(d) DATE
(b) Time in Grade	(b) Sharpshooter	
(c) SQT score (59 or below)	(c) Marksman	

(3) Most recent Physical Fitness Test Scores (Minimum score of 60 in each event.)	(4) (a) SOLDIER'S CURRENT SQT SCORE	(4) (b) DATE
(a) Situps	(5) I certify (Must check one of the following on all recommendations):	
(b) Pushups		
(c) Two-Mile Run	(a) That the soldier has taken an SQT during the most recent test period.	
(d) Total (e) DATE	(b) That the soldier has not taken an SQT due to no fault of his/her own.	
14. REMARKS	(c) That the soldier failed to take an SQT during the most recent test period due to his/her own fault.	
	(6) PROMOTION POINTS AWARDED TO SOLDIER FOR DUTY PERFORMANCE (Maximum 200 points)	

15a. SIGNATURE BLOCK OF COMMANDER	15b. SIGNATURE OF COMMANDER	15c. DATE
16a. SIGNATURE BLOCK OF PROMOTION AUTHORITY	16b. SIGNATURE OF PROMOTION AUTHORITY	16c. CHECK ONE ☐ Approved ☐ Disapproved 16d. DATE

SECTION B - ADMINISTRATIVE POINTS

	POINTS GRANTED
1. DUTY PERFORMANCE - MAXIMUM 200 POINTS (Enter points awarded by Commander for duty performance on promotion recommendation (See Section A, item (13b(6).)	
2. SKILL QUALIFICATION TEST (SQT) - MAXIMUM 200 POINTS	POINTS GRANTED
a. Enter the soldier's latest SQT score from the Individual Soldier's Report (ISR), or TSO data, if the score is 60 or higher → x 2 =	
b. Enter the number of promotion points granted under the no fault provision.	

DA FORM 3355, APR 91   DA FORM 3355, MAR 85 IS OBSOLETE   USAPPC V2.00

3. Awards and Decorations - *Maximum 50 Points.* List and multiply the number of awards received by the number of points authorized for the award as explained in the instructions.

	x	=		x	=		x	=
	x	=		x	=		x	=
	x	=		x	=		x	=

Total Points Granted ⟶

4. Military Education - *Maximum 150 Points*

5. Civilian Education - *Maximum 100 Points*						6. Military Training - *Maximum 100 Points*	
						a. Marksmanship	
						b. Physical Fitness Test	
Total Points Granted ⟶						c. Total Points ⟶	

7. I certify that the above administrative points shown have been accurately extracted from appropriate records and promotion points indicated are correct.

a. SIGNATURE OF RESPONSIBLE OFFICIAL	b. GRADE	c. DATE	d. SIGNATURE OF RECOMMENDED INDIVIDUAL

SECTION C - TOTALS

Note - *Only the fractional total promotion points in item 3 of this section will be rounded off to the nearest whole number. A fraction of 5/10 or higher will be rounded up to the next higher whole number. A fraction of 4/10 or less will be rounded down to the next lowest whole number.*	GRANTED
1. TOTAL ADMINISTRATIVE POINTS - *MAXIMUM 800 POINTS (Total of items 1 through 6, Section B.)*	
2. TOTAL BOARD POINTS - *MAXIMUM 200 POINTS*	
3. TOTAL PROMOTION POINTS - *MAXIMUM 1,000 POINTS (Add items 1 and 2.)*	

4. I certify that the total points shown have been accurately extracted from appropriate records and promotion list points indicated are correct.

a. SIGNATURE OF BOARD RECORDER	b. GRADE	c. DATE

5. I certify that the soldier has been recommended for promotion by a valid promotion board.

a. SIGNATURE BLOCK OF PROMOTION AUTHORITY	b. SIGNATURE	c. DATE BOARD PROCEEDINGS WERE APPROVED

6. STATEMENT *(Use only when a recommendation is disapproved, when a soldier is not selected by the board, or when the soldier cannot be added to the recommended list due to not attaining the minimum required points.)*

"I have been counseled on my promotion status and deficiencies."

a. SIGNATURE OF SOLDIER	b. DATE	c. TYPED OR PRINTED NAME OF COUNSELOR
		d. SIGNATURE OF COUNSELOR

D. Air Force Enlisted Performance Reports

ENLISTED PERFORMANCE REPORT (AB thru TSGT)

I. RATEE IDENTIFICATION DATA *(Read AFI 36-2403 carefully before completing any item)*

1. NAME *(Last, First, Middle Initial)*	2. SSN	3. GRADE	4. DAFSC

5. ORGANIZATION, COMMAND, AND LOCATION	6a. PAS CODE	6b. SRID

7. PERIOD OF REPORT From:　　　Thru:	8. NO. DAYS SUPERVISION	9. REASON FOR REPORT

II. JOB DESCRIPTION

1. DUTY TITLE

2. KEY DUTIES, TASKS, AND RESPONSIBILITIES

III. EVALUATION OF PERFORMANCE

1. HOW WELL DOES RATEE PERFORM ASSIGNED DUTIES? *(Consider quality, quantity, and timeliness of duties performed)*

☐ Inefficient. An unprofessional performer.	☐ Good performer. Performs routine duties satisfactorily.	☐ Excellent performer. Consistently produces high quality work.	☐ The exception. Absolutely superior in all areas.

2. HOW MUCH DOES RATEE KNOW ABOUT PRIMARY DUTIES? *(Consider whether ratee has technical expertise and is able to apply the knowledge)*

☐ Does not have the basic knowledge necessary to perform duties.	☐ Has adequate technical knowledge to satisfactorily perform duties.	☐ Extensive knowledge of all primary duties and related positions.	☐ Excels in knowledge of all related positions. Mastered all duties.

3. HOW WELL DOES RATEE COMPLY WITH STANDARDS? *(Consider dress and appearance, weight and fitness, customs, and courtesies)*

☐ Fails to meet minimum standards.	☐ Meets Air Force standards.	☐ Sets the example for others to follow.	☐ Exemplifies top military standards.

4. HOW IS RATEE'S CONDUCT ON/OFF DUTY? *(Consider financial responsibility, respect for authority, support for organizational activities, and maintenance of government facilities)*

☐ Unacceptable.	☐ Acceptable.	☐ Sets the example for others.	☐ Exemplifies the standard of conduct.

5. HOW WELL DOES RATEE SUPERVISE/LEAD? *(Consider how well member sets and enforces standards, displays initiative and self-confidence, provides guidance and feedback, and fosters teamwork)*

☐ Ineffective.	☐ Effective. Obtains satisfactory results.	☐ Highly effective.	☐ Exceptionally effective leader.

6. HOW WELL DOES RATEE COMPLY WITH INDIVIDUAL TRAINING REQUIREMENTS? *(Consider upgrade training, professional military education, proficiency/qualification, and contingency)*

☐ Does not comply with minimum training requirements.	☐ Complies with most training requirements.	☐ Complies with all training requirements.	☐ Consistently exceeds all training requirements.

7. HOW WELL DOES RATEE COMMUNICATE WITH OTHERS? *(Consider ratee's verbal and written skills)*

☐ Unable to express thoughts clearly. Lacks organization.	☐ Organizes and expresses thoughts satisfactorily.	☐ Consistently able to organize and express ideas clearly and concisely.	☐ Highly skilled writer and communicator.

AF FORM 910, JUN 95 *(EF-V2) (PerFORM PRO)*   PREVIOUS EDITIONS ARE OBSOLETE.

IV. PROMOTION RECOMMENDATION *(Compare this ratee with others of the same grade and AFS)*

RECOMMENDATION	NOT RECOMMENDED	NOT RECOMMENDED AT THIS TIME	CONSIDER	READY	IMMEDIATE PROMOTION
RATER'S RECOMMENDATION	1	2	3	4	5
INDORSER'S RECOMMENDATION	1	2	3	4	5

V. RATER'S COMMENTS

I certify that in accordance with AFI 36-2403 an initial feedback session was conducted on _____, and a midterm feedback session was conducted on _____. *(If not accomplished, state the reason).*

NAME, GRADE, BR OF SVC, ORGN, COMD & LOCATION	DUTY TITLE		DATE
	SSN	SIGNATURE	

VI. INDORSER'S COMMENTS   CONCUR   NONCONCUR

NAME, GRADE, BR OF SVC, ORGN, COMD & LOCATION	DUTY TITLE		DATE
	SSN	SIGNATURE	

INSTRUCTIONS

Reports written by a senior rater or the Chief Master Sergeant of the Air Force (CMSAF) will not be indorsed.

Reports written by colonels or civilians (GM-15 or higher) do not require an indorser; however, indorsement is permitted unless prohibited by the instruction above.

When the rater's rater is not at least a MSgt or civilian (GS-07 or higher), the indorser is the next official in the rating chain serving in the grade of MSgt or higher, or a civilian in the grade of GS-07 or higher.

When the final evaluator (rater or indorser) is not an Air Force officer or a DAF civilian, an Air Force advisor review is required.

VII. COMMANDER'S REVIEW

CONCUR	NONCONCUR *(Attach AF Form 77)*	SIGNATURE

AF FORM 910, JUN 95 *(REVERSE) (EF-V2) (PerFORM PRO)*

SENIOR ENLISTED PERFORMANCE REPORT *(MSGT thru CMSGT)*

I. RATEE IDENTIFICATION DATA *(Read AFI36-2403 carefully before completing any item)*

1. NAME *(Last, First, Middle Initial)*	2. SSN	3. GRADE	4. DAFSC

5. ORGANIZATION, COMMAND, AND LOCATION	6a. PAS CODE	6b. SRID

7. PERIOD OF REPORT From: Thru:	8. NO. DAYS SUPERVISION	9. REASON FOR REPORT

II. JOB DESCRIPTION

1. DUTY TITLE

2. KEY DUTIES, TASKS, AND RESPONSIBILITIES

III. EVALUATION OF PERFORMANCE

1. DUTY PERFORMANCE *(Consider quality, quantity, and timeliness of duties performed)*

☐ Inefficient. An unprofessional performer.	☐ Good performer. Performs routine duties satisfactorily.	☐ Excellent performer. Consistently produces high quality work.	☐ The exception. Absolutely superior in all areas.

2. JOB KNOWLEDGE *(Consider whether ratee has technical expertise and is able to apply the knowledge)*

☐ Lacking. Needs considerable improvement.	☐ Sufficient. Gets job accomplished.	☐ Extensive knowledge of all primary duties and related positions.	☐ Excels in knowledge of all related positions. Mastered all duties.

3. LEADERSHIP *(Consider whether ratee motivates peers or subordinates, maintains discipline, sets and enforces standards, evaluates subordinates fairly and consistently, plans and organizes work, and fosters teamwork)*

☐ Ineffective.	☐ Gets satisfactory results.	☐ Highly effective leader.	☐ Exceptionally effective leader.

4. MANAGERIAL SKILLS *(Consider how well member uses time and resources)*

☐ Ineffective.	☐ Manages resources in a satisfactory manner.	☐ Skillful and competent.	☐ Dynamic, capitalizes on all opportunities.

5. JUDGEMENT *(Consider how well ratee evaluates situations and reaches logical conclusions)*

☐ Poor.	☐ Sound.	☐ Emphasizes logic and decision making.	☐ Highly respected and skilled.

6. PROFESSIONAL QUALITIES *(Consider ratee's dedication and preservation of traditional military values - integrity and loyalty)*

☐ Unprofessional, unreliable.	☐ Meets expectations.	☐ Sets an example for others to follow.	☐ Epitomizes the Air Force professional.

7. COMMUNICATION SKILLS *(Consider ratee's ability to organize and express ideas)*

☐ Unable to communicate effectively.	☐ Organizes and expresses thoughts satisfactorily.	☐ Organizes and expresses ideas clearly and concisely.	☐ Highly skilled writer and communicator.

AF FORM 911, JUN 95 *(EF-V2)* *(PerFORM PRO)*   PREVIOUS EDITIONS ARE OBSOLETE.

IV. PROMOTION RECOMMENDATION
(Compare this ratee with others of the same grade and AFS. For CMSgts, this is a recommendation for increased responsibilities.)

RECOMMENDATION	NOT RECOMMENDED	NOT RECOMMENDED AT THIS TIME	CONSIDER	READY	IMMEDIATE PROMOTION
RATER'S RECOMMENDATION	1	2	3	4	5
RATER'S RATER'S RECOMMENDATION	1	2	3	4	5

V. RATER'S COMMENTS

I certify that in accordance with AFI 36-2403 an initial feedback session was conducted on _____, and a midterm feedback session was conducted on _____. *(If not accomplished, state the reason).*

NAME, GRADE, BR OF SVC, ORGN, COMD & LOCATION	DUTY TITLE		DATE
	SSN	SIGNATURE	

VI. RATER'S RATER'S COMMENTS   CONCUR   NONCONCUR

NAME, GRADE, BR OF SVC, ORGN, COMD & LOCATION	DUTY TITLE		DATE
	SSN	SIGNATURE	

VII. INDORSER'S COMMENTS   CONCUR   NONCONCUR

NAME, GRADE, BR OF SVC, ORGN, COMD & LOCATION	DUTY TITLE		DATE
	SSN	SIGNATURE	

VIII. FINAL EVALUATOR'S POSITION		IX. TIME-IN-GRADE ELIGIBLE *(N/A for CMSgt or CMSgt selectee)*		X. COMMANDER'S REVIEW	
A	SENIOR RATER			CONCUR	NONCONCUR *(Attach AF Form 77)*
B	SENIOR RATER'S DEPUTY			SIGNATURE	
C	INTERMEDIATE LEVEL	YES			
D	LOWER LEVEL	NO			

AF FORM 911, JUN 95 *(REVERSE) (EF-V2) (PerFORM PRO)*